The

Biblical Case

for

BREXIT

Pastor Peter Simpson

Righteousness exalteth a nation: but sin is a reproach to any people.

(Proverbs 14:34)

The

Biblical Case

for

BREXIT

Why Britain should leave the European Union and return to its historic Christian foundations

An expanded version of the original 12-page A5 booklet of the same title

Pastor Peter Simpson

Belmont House Publishing

London

The Biblical Case for BREXIT

Published by Belmont House Publishing Ltd
First published April 2016

ISBN 978 0 9954845 0 4

© Copyright 2016. Pastor Peter Simpson.
revps@icloud.com; 01494 812829

The right of Peter Simpson to be identified as the author of this work has been asserted by him.

Penn Free Methodist Church Publications

Scripture quotations are from the Authorised (King James) Version of the Bible, the rights of which are vested in the Crown and administered by the Crown's patentee, Cambridge University Press.

Published by Belmont House Publishing, 36 The Crescent, Belmont, Sutton, Surrey, SM2 6BJ

A catalogue of this book is available from the British Library.

Contents

Introduction   **1**

1) Britain must leave the EU because membership is a secular nation's substitute for trusting in God.   **2**

2) Britain must leave the EU because membership makes impossible proper border controls, which are a Biblical responsibility.   **3**

3) Britain must leave the EU because membership means taking on the financial obligations of others contrary to Biblical principles.   **6**

4) Britain must leave the EU because membership is incompatible with its Christian and Bible-based constitution.   **8**

5) Britain must leave the EU because membership provides no guarantee of peace between nations.   **10**

6) Britain must leave the EU because membership is incompatible with the God-ordained institution of nationhood.   **12**

Conclusion   **14**

Introduction

Britain is approaching a referendum on its membership of the European Union (EU). How should Christians vote? Whilst we acknowledge that there will be sincere Christian people who will support EU membership, and whilst we assert our brotherly respect for all such, we nevertheless contend that the Biblical evidence for leaving the EU is overwhelming.

To speak out on this issue is not a question of the churches foolishly getting involved in politics. This matter transcends politics and is about God's purpose for a fallen world and for the arrangement of human societies. It is about our destiny as a people. It is about what a nation is trusting in for its security and well-being.

The debate is being conducted in entirely secular terms, and economic issues are playing an enormous role. However, it is absolutely essential that the issue of God's providence is brought into the discussion. The voters must be told that it is the Trinitarian God who is the Ruler of the nations and to whom governments are answerable:

*Come and see the works of God... He ruleth by his power for ever; his eyes behold the nations (*Psalms 66:5,7).

"I blessed the most High, and I praised and honoured him that liveth for ever, whose dominion is an everlasting dominion... he doeth according to his will in the army of heaven, and among the inhabitants of the earth: and none can stay his hand, or say unto him, What doest thou? (Daniel 4:34–35).

1. Britain must leave the EU because membership is a secular nation's substitute for trusting in God.

When Britain joined the Common Market in 1973, it was a nation afflicted by economic crises and industrial turmoil (Edward Heath had to declare no less than 5 states of emergency during his premiership).[1] The God-rejecting 'permissive society' was also transforming our culture. In 1969 the then Chancellor of the Exchequer had described permissiveness as the mark of a civilised society.[2] This revealed the extent to which secular liberalism was, by then, destroying our nation's Christian identity.

By 1973 people were increasingly accustomed to frequent television watching, where they would be drip-fed the new creed of 'do your own thing', as the boundaries of what was morally acceptable were constantly being pushed out. In 1974 another society-transforming assault upon Biblical values took place: family planning clinics were given the go-ahead to prescribe the contraceptive pill to unmarried mothers.[3] More generally, the doctrines of cultural Marxism were now being so widely propagated that most people would soon simply lose the will to resist. The very few like Mary Whitehouse who did dare to protest were ridiculed as humorous relics from the past.

So as Britain voted to remain in the European Economic Community in 1975, it was in the context of a society deliberately abandoning the decency and wholesomeness of a Bible-imbued culture. We were a nation despising itself and its history, and believing that the problems of the world were mainly a legacy of our nasty imperialistic past. Labour disputes were also crippling British industry at this time. The Protestant work ethic had become no more than a piece of historical quaintness. In short, Britain was in such a dejected and degenerate condition that it was ripe for a craven retreat into the arms of a foreign alliance, in the vain hope that there would be safety in numbers.

So membership of the European Economic Community became the focus of hope for a secularised people in their desire for national recovery. By now Britain was made up of a *generation which knew not the LORD, nor yet the works which he had done* (Judges 2:10). Because of this, we resorted to Europe for survival, precisely because the concept of trusting in the God who governs the nations had become beyond our secular comprehension. Britain now knew nothing of the Biblical teaching that national prosperity is intricately connected to obedience to the one true God (for example, in Deuteronomy 28:1-14). So the UK's involvement in the European project became a secularist insurance policy, indeed a crutch, for a God-rejecting people, in contrast to the scriptural principle of :

> *Put not your trust in princes, nor in the son of man, in whom there is no help* (Psalm 146:3).

2. Britain must leave the EU because membership makes impossible proper border controls, which are a Biblical responsibility.

The need to respect national boundaries is clearly taught in Scripture. It is implicit in the injunctions of the law of Moses to respect tribal and family boundaries, for example:

> *Thou shalt not remove thy neighbour's landmark* (Deuteronomy 19:14).

The integrity of national boundaries is plainly set forth in Numbers 20 and 21, where we read of the Israelites travelling from the wilderness to the Promised Land. They needed to pass through the territory belonging to the Edomites and the Amorites. So they asked the kings of those two nations for permission. Moses told the kings that his people would not stray from the main highway, nor touch any crops. He even offered to pay for any water that Israel's cattle consumed in transit. He thus carefully observed the Edomites' and Amorites' boundaries as being ordained of God, and worthy of all respect.

Let us now consider the current situation regarding control of our borders. 617,000 people migrated into Britain in the year to September 2015; the net figure was 323,000, of which 257,000 were from EU.[4] This follows a gross influx of 636,000 in the year to June 2015.[5] The Migration Watch UK organisation reports, in an extrapolation from recent immigration statistics, that "the population is projected to rise by 500,000 a year and so reach 73 million" by 2030, a rise of nearly 8 million.[6] Where are all these incomers going to live? Such levels of immigration are quite unsustainable in terms of the functioning of public services, the maintenance of the infrastructure and the conservation of the countryside, including productive agricultural land. England is already one of the most crowded countries on the planet and is the most densely populated European country, except for Malta.[7]

British membership of the EU makes it far more difficult for the Government to control immigration properly, because people from 27 other countries are free to come to Britain to find employment. Is such a situation fair to those Britons who are looking for work and who do not wish to leave their own land in order to find it? Why should they have to compete in their own country with many others from abroad?

Migration Watch further reports that "the economic benefit of EU migration has been greatly exaggerated, especially in respect of East Europeans who are mostly in low paid employment".[8] It also states, "The number of EU nationals working in the UK has increased by 215,000 in the year to Quarter 4, 2015".[9] As many of these EU workers will be at the lower-paid end of the labour market, Britons looking for work at the same lower wage levels will face increasing competition for the available posts. They will also be suffering from downward pressure on their wages because of the wide availability of migrant labour.

In 2015, 630,000 EU citizens registered for a UK National Insurance number.[10] From June 2011 to June 2015 around 2.2 million NI numbers were handed out to migrants from the EU.[11] Such levels of influx must not automatically be regarded by Christians as somehow being virtuous in God's sight. There is nothing remotely wrong with a national government putting the needs of its own citizens first, any more than it is wrong for a father in managing his income and household to put the needs of his own family first.

There is a great danger in Christians thinking that they must not make immigration a factor when considering the issue of Britain's EU membership. This is mainly because of the vast influence of secular political correctness within the churches. The Archbishop of Canterbury, Justin Welby, has stated:

> *At the heart of Christian teaching about the human being is that all human beings are of absolutely equal and infinite value, and the language we use must reflect the value of the human being and not treat immigration as just a deep menace that is somehow going to overwhelm a country that has coped with many waves of immigration.*[12]

We respond politely that this statement seriously misses the mark, because the equality of all peoples has absolutely nothing to do with a discussion about nation-transforming levels of migration. No one supporting tighter border controls is remotely arguing that immigrants are of less value as human beings. More recently the Archbishop has rightly stated that to be fearful about the consequences of mass migration is not racist[13] – and we welcome that – but he also speaks approvingly in the same interview of Germany taking in 1.1 million migrants in 2015.[14] which suggests that he is far from withdrawing the comments quoted above. In regard to the great influx into Germany, an EU commissioner has stated that many of the incomers are not actually from Syria, and so have not been fleeing from war.[15] In an EU context Chancellor Merkel's decision to welcome such an enormous number of migrants inevitably affects other member nations, quite simply because of geography, and also because the EU sets such great store upon the free movement of peoples as a core principle.

For the last 50 years the churches have consistently taken a pro-immigration stance, arguing that the levels of immigration sustained by Britain historically are comparable to the levels experienced since the 1960s to the present day. Such a comparison, however, is quite untenable, because it ignores facts such as: a) in the decade from 2001 to 2011 the Government allowed the population, through immigration, to grow at a faster rate than at any time since the first ever census conducted in 1801;[16] b) 3.6 million migrants entered the UK between 1997 and 2010;[17] c) year on year net migration is now running at 300,000 plus;[18] d) in 2014 Britain was accommodating 565,000 schoolchildren from European migrant families, and this figure rose in 2015 to 699,000.[19]

There is no immigration in our long history which is anywhere near the levels indicated in these figures. So our point quite simply is that membership of the EU makes it far more difficult for Britain to control its borders (and this seems to be hard enough anyway), because nearly 450 million people from other member states now have automatic right of access into the UK. We assert most strongly that as Christians we love our neighbour, whoever he is and wherever he comes from, but that does not mean that we must ignore the difficulties which large-scale immigration brings, such as wage depression amongst the lower paid, pressures on public services and the cultural transformation of neighbourhoods.

3. Britain must leave the EU because membership means taking on the financial obligations of others contrary to Biblical principles.

The cost of Britain's membership is over £14.3 billion p.a., of which we receive back less than 50%.[20] This means that the UK is helping to subsidise many other foreign governments. This is contrary to the Biblical principle of ensuring that one remains personally responsible before God for the stewardship of one's own assets, and does not assume liability for the debts and financial actions of others over whose actions one has no control.

We read in Proverbs 11:15, *He that is surety for a stranger shall smart for it: and he that hateth suretiship is sure.*

The Hebrew word translated 'stranger' in this verse can sometimes mean a foreigner, sometimes one who is not a member of one's own grouping, and sometimes simply any other individual. Thus the word of God is telling us, Do not take on the role of surety as a general rule. 'To be surety' for another means to make his financial obligations and his possible unwise conduct one's own responsibility. In its membership of the EU Britain is doing just that – taking on the financial liabilities of others.

We see the 'surety' principle in the European Financial Stability Mechanism (EFSM). This is a special fund to help ailing economies within the EU. The EFSM "is funded by borrowing against the EU budget, to which the UK contributes".[21] Through this fund Britain could be put into a position of having to guarantee loans to other member nations which are in grave economic difficulties. This arrangement is a direct breach of the principle set out in Proverbs 11:15.

Also, by being a net contributor to the EU budget, the UK is taking on a financial liability concerning the actions of the European Commission and other national governments, over which it has little control. Britain is thus making herself a 'surety', or guarantor, for the economic well-being of the net recipient member nations, in contradiction of the Biblical warning against such a role. A further text states:

If thou be surety... thou art snared with the words of thy mouth (Proverbs 6:1-2).

This counsel to individuals applies equally to nations. How unwise it is to act as a financial guarantor to other nations, when there is no ability to influence the policies which they carry out, which policies may even be diametrically opposed to those of the UK Government.

A further example of Britain's acting as guarantor to other nations is seen in the events of October 2014, when the UK Government was told it had to contribute a further £1.7bn into the EU budget precisely because of the British economy's good performance.[22] The Government subsequently conceded to this demand.[23] So Britain was required to pay more from its own resources into the EU coffers, to compensate for member nations whose economies had not performed so well as her own. This is none other than taking on the role of 'surety' for other EU nations.

At the time of writing it is further being proposed within the EU that there be a common fund set up into which all EU members will pay in order to help support the jobless within the Eurozone at times of financial crisis and high unemployment.[24] The concept behind this proposed fund is that the Union as a whole will share the economic risks of all its constituent members.

This indeed has always been the ethos of the European project, and it is why Britain has always been a net contributor to the EU budget (putting more in than we receive back). Such an ethos, however, represents an abandonment of the wisdom of God's word, which teaches that it is reckless to assume the financial obligations of others whose actions one cannot control. Just as each individual is personally answerable to God for the propriety of his financial dealings, so must it be with nations.

4. Britain must leave the EU because membership is incompatible with its Christian and Bible-based constitution.

The constitution of the EU, which was agreed upon back in 2004, lacks any specific reference to the Trinitarian God and the Christian faith. The preamble to the constitution merely refers to "the cultural, religious and humanist inheritance of Europe, from which have developed the universal values of the inviolable and inalienable rights of the human person, freedom, democracy, equality and the rule of law".[25] The vague term 'religious' avoids the word 'Christian', and we are left with the idea that secular culture and humanism have contributed just as much, or even more, to European civilisation as Christianity may have done, and these secular contributory sources presumably include even the anti-Christian French Revolution.

So the EU has chosen to make no formal identification with the Christian faith. How could it, and then encourage strongly Islamic Turkey to join? This is in stark contrast to the British constitution, where there is a definitive acknowledgement of the teachings of the Christian Scriptures. Furthermore, our head of state is actually required by existing statute law (the 1688 Coronation Oath Act) "to the utmost of her power to maintain the laws of God and the true profession of the gospel".[26] In the coronation service in 1953 the Moderator of the General Assembly of the Church of Scotland presented to the Queen a copy of the Bible, as the following words were spoken:

> *To keep your Majesty ever mindful of the law and the gospel of God as the rule for the whole life and government of Christian princes, we present you with this Book, the most valuable thing that this world affords.*[27]

That our head of state is installed into her office in such a manner represents a glorious national heritage. It means that the word of God, His own revelation of Himself, has been placed at the centre of our national life. We reject this constitutional privilege as being an irrelevant archaism at our peril.

Under the British constitution there also exist national churches established by law. This speaks of a distinct identification with Biblical Christianity which is contrary to the spirit of the EU constitution. Furthermore, the original historic doctrinal statement of the Church of England includes an article which, if adhered to, would immediately render invalid this nation's membership of the EU:

> *The Queen's Majesty hath the chief power in this realm... and is not, nor ought to be, subject to any foreign jurisdiction*[28] (Article 37 of the 39 Articles).

5. Britain must leave the EU because membership provides no guarantee of peace between nations.

Many people argue that it is necessary for Britain to remain within the EU because it has been responsible for maintaining peace within Europe since the end of the Second World War. This contention must be hotly disputed, for it is membership of NATO which has been the crucial factor in Britain and Europe's security, and this membership has not required the abandonment of national sovereignty.

In any case, from a Christian perspective, we know that it is the providence of God which determines whether or not a nation will experience peace, not the alliances which men endeavour to form. Between 1943 and 1992 Yugoslavia comprised an alliance of nations, but that political union did not guarantee peace amongst its constituent parts, but eventually resulted in a series of horrific conflicts and the creation of separate nation states.[29]

The point for us to grasp is that national well-being and prosperity, including the absence of war, are functions of a nation's standing with God. We read in 2 Chronicles 14:

> *Asa did that which was good and right in the eyes of the Lord his God… and commanded Judah to seek the Lord God of their fathers* (2 Chronicles 14:2,4).

So Asa, King of Judah, opposed false religion and led the nation back to the worship of the one true God. The consequence of this was:

> *The kingdom was quiet before him… the land had rest, and he had no war in those years; because the LORD had given him rest* (2 Chronicles 14:5-6).

So we see clearly that it was the Lord who brought peace to Judah. Subsequently, however, King Asa failed to keep on trusting God for the nation's security. When conflict arose with the northern kingdom of Israel, he resorted to forming a treaty with Syria. He denuded the Temple and royal palace of much of their gold and silver, so as to pass the proceeds on to the Syrians, as an allurement to their becoming allies.

Let us note here the unwholesome principle of large financial contributions going out of the country in order to secure a foreign alliance, and that at the root of this situation there was *spiritual* declension in high places in Judah – a rejection of God, rather than it simply being a military or political problem.

The Lord responded to Asa's faithlessness by sending a prophet to him. We are told in 2 Chronicles 16:

> *Hanani the seer came to Asa king of Judah, and said unto him... Thou hast relied on the king of Syria, and not relied on the Lord thy God... Herein thou hast done foolishly: therefore from henceforth thou shalt have wars. Then Asa was wroth with the seer, and put him in a prison house* (2 Chronicles 16:7,9,10).

Let us observe here that the nation which turns its back on God and seeks instead to cultivate foreign alliances does not ultimately prosper. The prophet Hanani actually told the king that more wars were going to afflict Judah in the future, despite her alliance with Syria. This again teaches us that, whilst men act sinfully of their own volition in starting wars, the conflicts nevertheless occur in the providence of God.

If, in any period of history, a nation is free from war, it is because the Trinitarian God has chosen to bless the nation in that manner. We today, therefore, must have the courage to shout from the housetops the vital doctrine of God's providential government over the nations, as we consider the future direction which Britain is to take.

We must not think that freedom from war will be guaranteed by membership of the European Union, as many are arguing. The abolition of the nation state is not the answer to the problems of the world. What is needed is the transformation of man's corrupted heart. Only the Christian gospel can achieve this, and thereby begin to make a nation righteous, and thus less liable to both internal and external conflict.

6. Britain must leave the EU because membership is incompatible with the God-ordained institution of nationhood.

Britain's EU membership contradicts the very ordinance of God. In Deuteronomy 32:8 Moses tells us that, just as the Lord separated the nation of Israel, so He also ordained the independent existence of all the other nations:

The most High divided to the nations their inheritance...
he set the bounds of the people.

So here is God's own stamp upon the legitimacy of nationhood and national borders. This legitimacy is re-endorsed in the New Testament, where we read in Acts 17:26:

(God) hath made of one blood all nations of men for to
dwell on all the face of the earth, and hath determined...
the bounds of their habitation.

The divine institution of nationhood goes back to Genesis chapter 10, where we read of "the generations of the sons of Noah, Shem, Ham and Japheth" who would form the basis of the various different nations in the future history of the world following the global flood.

Those nations, however, did not immediately come into being, for in Genesis 11 we read of all the peoples then living as not yet being in distinctive national groups, but rather as rebelling against such a prospect, and rebelling against the authority of God generally. Nimrod was the leader of this rebellion.

They said, Go to, let us build us a city and a tower,
whose top may reach unto heaven; and let us make us
a name, lest we be scattered abroad upon the face of
the whole earth (Genesis 11:4).

Satanic inspired false religion had taken hold of these people. They turned to the worship of the stars and other created objects, and the tower of Babel was an idolatrous temple built in honour of the heavenly spheres.

In defiance of their Maker the people were refusing to spread out across the earth to form separate nations, which was God's purpose for them. Instead, they desired to create a single world empire whose strength lay in its human solidarity. God therefore confounded their languages, so that they had no choice but to disperse into separate units on the basis of their tongues.

So we see from this early phase of human history that the Lord was actually imposing nationhood because of mankind's wayward behaviour. Because all men are fallen and in rebellion against God, nationhood is God's chosen method of ordering His world.

Under the new covenant the Lord has never rescinded His decree given at the time of the Tower of Babel that rebellious fallen men, because of their propensity to unite in hostility against Him, should be scattered over the earth into different language groups and nations (Genesis 11:8). This has a direct bearing upon the current debate on Britain's EU membership, because that membership unequivocally erodes national sovereignty and self-determination.

Now we read in Genesis 30:25:

> *It came to pass, when Rachel had born Joseph, that Jacob said unto Laban, Send me away, that I may go unto mine own place, and to my country.*

Here we see Jacob desiring to return to the land of his birth. He calls it "his own place". He has been living in Mesopotamia for 14 years, but Canaan is still "his own place". So we see here a man of God speaking of the reality of his national identity and native affiliation.

Jacob's return to Canaan was of course all part of the unfolding of God's plan of salvation for mankind, a plan which centred upon the very institution of nationhood. Indeed, for 2000 years from the time of Abraham God would specifically use nationhood in the working out of His glorious scheme of redemption for the world. This fact alone proves that nationhood cannot be intrinsically wrong or morally defective.

Let us make no mistake, the Bible plainly teaches that God Himself has ordained nationhood and clearly defined national boundaries. John Wesley once wrote, "We feel in ourselves a strong… kind of natural affection for our country, which we apprehend Christianity was never designed either to root out or to impair".[30] What a wonderfully non-pc statement: Christianity was never designed to destroy a sense of national identity!

Conclusion

As Bible-believing Christians we do not present 'Brexit' as a panacea for the nation's ills. We believe it to be very necessary, but it must also be accompanied by the preaching of the gospel of personal salvation, and by a nationwide turning in repentance and faith to the only Saviour of men, the Lord Jesus Christ.

It is vital that those who adhere to the authority of God's word are not afraid to use theological arguments when advocating Britain's departure from the EU. The Government has distributed a taxpayer-funded booklet to households throughout the UK in support of our remaining in the Union. This booklet emphasises that "EU membership brings economic security, peace and stability".[31] A generalisation such as this must be challenged on theological grounds, because it pays no regard to the providence of God, which, the Bible teaches, is alone responsible for how a nation fares in terms of its general prosperity. A key verse in this regard is Proverbs 14:34:

> *Righteousness exalteth a nation: but sin is a reproach to any people.*

Britain's own history vividly illustrates this truth that God's providence is the determining factor in a nation's well-being. Our country in the early 18th century, for example, was characterised by social deprivation and disorder, by corruption in high places and by appalling working conditions. It was vigorous gospel preaching which gradually transformed this miserable situation. As the Cambridge historian, G. M. Trevelyan, observed, "(The) preaching of the Wesleys and Whitefield... deeply moved a vast mass of human beings hitherto neglected by Church and State... (there) began a new chapter in the religious, social and educational history of the working class. The coincidence in time of Wesley and the Industrial Revolution had profound effects... for generations to come".[32]

So the point which needs emphasising is that we must not idolise political and economic alliances as being the guarantors of peace and prosperity. God acts differently: He exalts the nation which honours Him. It is righteousness, not a skilfully crafted federation of nations, which will cause the country to prosper. In Old Testament times the prophets told Israel not to trust in foreign alliances, but in God alone. For example, we read in Isaiah:

> *Associate yourselves, O ye people, and ye shall be broken in pieces... Take counsel together, and it shall come to nought... Say ye not, A confederacy* (Isaiah 8:9,10,12).

God has not changed. He still judges nations as nations. The EU in our day cannot bring us peace and wealth. Britain must not foolishly seek safety in numbers. God is looking for righteousness before Him.

What is missing from the EU referendum debate is an appreciation of the doctrine of God's providence. We should remember that it was our present Queen's father who back in 1940 called for two national days of prayer at the time of the Dunkirk evacuation and the Battle of Britain. On both occasions the churches were packed, and God worked mighty national deliverances for us, confirming the truth that it is the providence of God which determines the destiny and well-being of nations.

The apostle Paul, after his conversion to Christ, never lost his sense of identity with his own people. He remained a Jew through and through.

He poured out his heart to God in concern for his own countrymen. Jeremiah did the same thing. He cried out:

Oh that my head were waters, and mine eyes a fountain of tears, that I might weep day and night for the slain of the daughter of my people! (Jeremiah 9:1).

How Britain today needs Christians with a similar Spirit-given burden for their nation such as Paul and Jeremiah possessed. Let us make no mistake, the Bible plainly teaches that God has ordained nationhood and clearly defined national boundaries. To reject this Divine ordinance because of secular fashion is to promote a Tower-of-Babel-like alternative world order, and Christians should not be doing that.

What our country needs today, above all else, is, not absorption into a supranational union, but mighty preaching of the gospel of salvation from sin through faith in our Lord and Saviour Jesus Christ.

(Endnotes)

1. http://www.economist.com/node/17090761
2. http://news.bbc.co.uk/1/hi/uk_politics/2629445.stm
3. http://www.bbc.co.uk/news/uk-15984258
4. http://order-order.com/2016/02/25/migration-figures-everything-you-need-to-know/
5. http://www.ons.gov.uk/ons/rel/migration1/migration-statistics-quarterly-report/november-2015/sty-net-migration.html
6. http://www.migrationwatchuk.org/key-topics/population
7. http://www.dailymail.co.uk/news/article-2530125/This-worryingly-crowded-isle-England-officially-Europes-densely-packed-country.html
8. http://www.migrationwatchuk.org/key-topics/european-union
9. http://www.migrationwatchuk.org/press-release/437
10. http://www.dailymail.co.uk/news/article-3472949/David-Cameron-REFUSES-release-figures-prove-true-level-EU-migration-UK.html
11. http://www.thetimes.co.uk/edition/news/mystery-solved-in-migration-figures-mismatch-x96ntz8fp
12. http://www.telegraph.co.uk/news/uknews/immigration/11190730/Archbishop-of-Canterbury-condemns-politicians-who-view-immigration-as-a-deep-menace.html
13. https://www.politicshome.com/home-affairs-foreign-and-defence/articles/house/justin-welby-eu-debate-not-all-about-us-its-about
14. Ibid
15. http://www.express.co.uk/news/world/638208/Almost-two-thirds-of-refugees-entering-Europe-are-NOT-fleeing-war-EU-Commissioner-claims?_ga=1.94856537.41862543.1369231506
16. http://www.dailymail.co.uk/debate/article-2213866/Lord-Carey-When-politicians-realise-racist-actually-DO-immigration.html
17. http://www.dailymail.co.uk/debate/article-3051489/DAILY-MAIL-COMMENT-Immigration-issue-time-totally-ignored-major-parties.html
18. Ibid.
19. http://www.express.co.uk/news/uk/668476/Schools-European-Union-migrant-children-mass-influx
20. http://leave.eu/en/the-facts/on-money
21. http://www.bbc.co.uk/news/uk-politics-33532485

22   http://www.bbc.co.uk/news/business-29751124
23   http://www.theguardian.com/politics/2014/nov/07/uk-pays-full-eu-rebate-despite-osborne-claim-he-halved-it
24   http://www.express.co.uk/news/politics/638661/pay-benefits-EU-jobless-crazy-plan-Brussels
25   http://news.bbc.co.uk/1/shared/bsp/hi/pdfs/09_01_05_constitution.pdf
26   http://www.legislation.gov.uk/aep/WillandMar/1/6/section/III
27   http://www.oremus.org/liturgy/coronation/cor1953b.html
28   https://www.churchofengland.org/prayer-worship/worship/book-of-common-prayer/articles-of-religion.aspx#XXXVII
29   https://en.wikipedia.org/wiki/Breakup_of_Yugoslavia
30   Reasons against Separation from C of E, Works of Wesley CD, Providence House Publishers
31   Why the Government believes that voting to remain in the European Union is the best decision for the UK (HM Government)
32   G. M. Trevelyan, English Social History, Longmans, Green & Co, 1946, p362.

The Biblical Case for BREXIT

Printed in Great Britain
by Amazon